A BEACON • BIOGRAPHY

MUHAMMAD ALI

Pete DiPrimio

PURPLE TOAD
PUBLISHING

Printing   1   2   3   4   5   6   7   8   9

A Beacon Biography

Angelina Jolie
Big Time Rush
Carly Rae Jepsen
Drake
Ed Sheeran
Harry Styles of One Direction
Jennifer Lawrence
Kevin Durant
Lorde
Malala
Markus "Notch" Persson, Creator of Minecraft
Mo'ne Davis
Muhammad Ali
Neil deGrasse Tyson
Peyton Manning
Robert Griffin III (RG3)

Publisher's Cataloging-in-Publication Data
DiPrimio, Pete.
    Muhammad Ali / written by Pete DiPrimio.
        p. cm.
            Includes bibliographic references and index.
            ISBN 9781624691874
1. Ali, Muhammad, 1942—Juvenile literature. 2. Boxers (Sports)—United States—Biography—Juvenile literature. I. Series: Beacon Biographies Collection Two.
 GV1132.A4 2016
 796.83092
                                        Library of Congress Control Number: 2015941814

eBook ISBN: 9781624691881

ABOUT THE AUTHOR: Pete DiPrimio is an award-winning sportswriter for the *Fort Wayne [Indiana] News-Sentinel,* and a longtime freelance writer. He's been an adjunct lecturer for the National Sports Journalism Center at IUPU-Indianapolis and for Indiana University's School of Journalism. He is the author of three nonfiction books pertaining to Indiana University athletics, and more than 15 children's books. He is currently completing his first novel. Pete is also a fitness instructor, plus a tennis and racquetball enthusiast.

PUBLISHER'S NOTE: The data in this book has been researched in depth, and to the best of our knowledge is factual. Although every measure is taken to give an accurate account, Purple Toad Publishing makes no warranty of the accuracy of the information and is not liable for damages caused by inaccuracies. This story has not been authorized or endorsed by Muhammad Ali.

CONTENTS

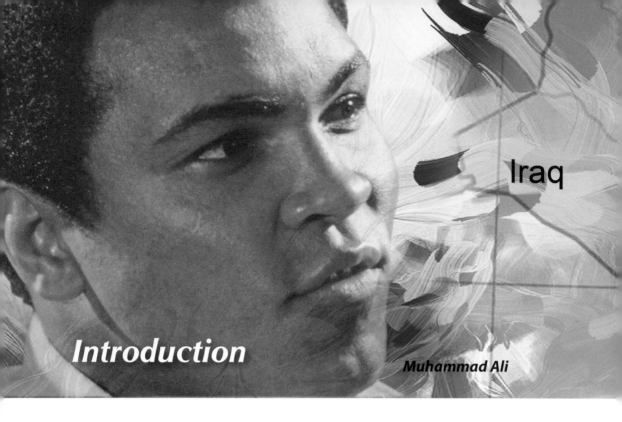

Iraq

Introduction

Muhammad Ali

It was 1990, and the United States was on the verge of war in the Middle East. An Iraqi dictator named Saddam Hussein had invaded the small country of Kuwait, and the world feared for its people.

Knowing America would not sit by and watch for long, Hussein took 15 innocent prisoners and chose to use them as human shields to keep American forces from sending missiles to stop him. The United Nations pleaded with him to release the helpless hostages, but after four months of negotiating with him, Hussein refused to free them. His plan was working; America could not act, and there was no one in the world who could reason with him.

But there is no one in the world quite like Muhammad Ali.

Years before, in 1981, a man in Los Angeles climbed out onto a ledge on the ninth floor of a building and threatened to jump. The police, a psychologist, and a minister tried to get the man down and failed. Then, out of nowhere came Muhammad Ali, the former World Boxing Champion, who offered his help to the police.

Ali went up the building, and soon came back down with the man. He had said to him, "You're my brother" and "I love you, I want to help you." When the man was safe on the ground, Ali said afterwards, "Saving a life is more important to me than winning a world championship."

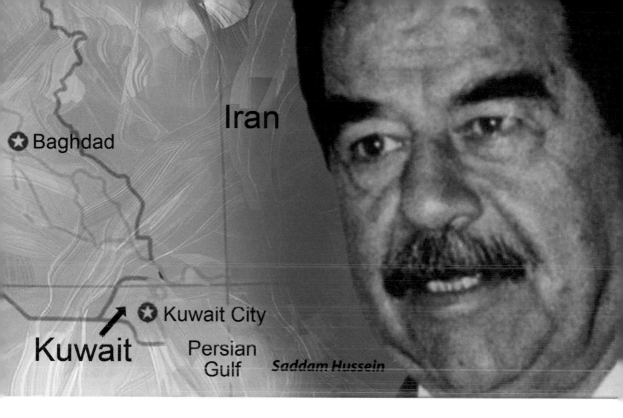

Iran

⭐ Baghdad

⭐ Kuwait City

Kuwait — Persian Gulf

Saddam Hussein

Now, the fate of 15 lives hung in the balance. A peace organization invited Muhammad Ali to Baghdad to try to meet with Hussein himself and to ask to free the hostages. They hoped the boxer's popularity there, as well as Ali being a Muslim, would be enough for Hussein to at least meet with him. While Ali waited in Baghdad for Hussein to decide to meet, he prayed in mosques, visited local schools, and met people on the streets. He did all this under the grip of Parkinson's disease, a progressive illness that causes shaking and weakness. He was on medication to help his speech and even to help him stand and walk.

The meeting finally took place and Ali met face to face with the feared Hussein about freeing the hostages. Ali knew he was putting himself at great risk, but he did not care. He asked Hussein to release the innocent people to him. After a lengthy and careful discussion, Hussein agreed, and after 4 long months of captivity, the 15 prisoners were given over to Ali to take home. When a hostage tried to thank him, Ali said, "God works through people. It's not me."

On December 3, they all arrived safely home, and Ali had reunited 15 grateful families. America would soon go to war, but on that day the world yet again called their hero Muhammad Ali, "The Greatest."

Cassius Clay began fighting at age 12. Six years later, he was an Olympic champion. Four years after that, he would stun the professional boxing world, change his name to Muhammad Ali, and make a lasting impact unlike any other.

Chapter

1

King of the World

Muhammad Ali tried to shadow box away his fear. He'd never been scared before in his boxing career. He was not afraid when he faced Tunney Hunsaker in his first professional fight, not afraid when he fought for an Olympic gold medal as a skinny teenager, and not afraid even when he laced up gloves for the first time at age 12.

But he had never faced anyone like Sonny Liston.

It was February 25, 1964, and Liston was the heavyweight champion of the world. He was also a convicted criminal who had spent two years in the Missouri State Penitentiary. He did not beat fighters as much as hurt them. He looked angry when he was happy. When he really was angry, his scowl could freeze a grizzly bear in its tracks.

Ali wasn't called Ali then. He was called Cassius Clay. Young, cocky, and talented, he fought like a lightweight. He "danced" around the ring (he later called it the "Ali shuffle"). He punched for the head instead of the body because he didn't like to get close enough to get hit. He didn't keep his hands up to protect his head because he was quick enough to dodge opponents' punches. Instead of slugging with power, he flashed quick jabs, again and again. One boxing official said, "He'll pick you and peck you, peck you and pick you, until you don't know where you are."

Clay talked so much that the words *The Lip* were stitched to the back of his white robe. Nearly every boxing expert picked Liston to knock him out, or worse. A *New York Times* reporter was told to find the fastest way to the nearest hospital from the Miami Beach Convention Hall boxing ring. That way the reporter could be there when Clay arrived.

Clay came in with an 18–0 record, but he had struggled in his previous two fights, almost getting knocked out in one of them. Liston was 35–1 and had been destroying everybody for years, including two first-round knockouts of former champ Floyd Patterson. He was a huge favorite.

Clay acted like he wasn't worried, but in private he was afraid that Liston would kill him. Liston had even joked a year earlier that if they fought, he might get jailed for murder. Still, Clay called Liston "the big, ugly bear" and predicted a knockout victory.

Clay trained hard, although he did make time to meet rock stars in a band called the Beatles, who had just come to America from England. A famous photo showed him pretending to knock them out. He was 22 years old and ready to shock the world.

The night of the fight, famous people mixed with mobsters around the ring. Entertainer Sammy Davis Jr. was there. So was Jackie Gleason, one of the world's best-known comedians. Gleason had predicted that "Blabber Mouth" would get knocked out in 13 seconds. Malcolm X, a civil rights leader, was there as Clay's guest and religious teacher. Surrounding them all was a thick haze of cigar smoke.

The fight began and Clay came out dancing, perfect for a fighter who described his style this way: "Float like a butterfly, sting like a bee." He was tall, graceful and threw punches faster than any heavyweight before him, perhaps faster than any fighter ever. Liston was shorter, stocky, and thickly muscled. He lumbered after Clay, tried cutting off the ring (use his body to stop Clay's dancing), and awkwardly threw a left jab that missed by two feet.

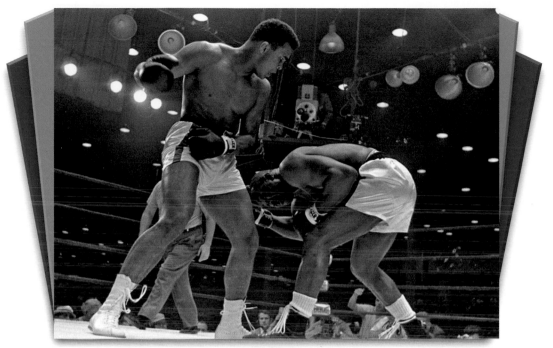

Sonny Liston had bullied his way to the heavyweight championship, but he couldn't bully Cassius Clay.

And so it went, round after round. Clay slashed at Liston's face with quick jabs. Liston grabbed and pushed and tried to set up a punch that would shut that mouth for good.

It never came.

At one point, ointment from Liston's gloves got into Clay's eyes. For a while, his eyes stung so bad he wanted to quit, but his corner men wouldn't let him.

In the sixth round, Clay hit Liston so often, the champ had had enough. He didn't come out for the seventh round, later claiming he'd hurt his shoulder. Clay ran around the ring, shouting, "I'm the king of the world!" He pointed at sportswriters who had predicted him to lose, saying, "Eat your words!"

The next day, Clay announced he was joining the Nation of Islam, and called himself Cassius X. A few weeks later, he changed his name to Muhammad Ali.

The world would never be the same.

Top left: Young Cassius (on right) and his brother Rudy. Top middle: The Clay family in the 1970s with Cassius, Rudy (he changed his name to Rahman Ali), mother Odessa and father Cassius Sr. Top right: Their Louisville home. Bottom: The bike (a Christmas present) that was stolen from Cassius when he was 12. A police officer, Joe Martin, helped him get it back, then invited the young Cassius for boxing lessons. Six weeks later, Cassius won his first fight.

Cassius Marcellus Clay Jr. was born on January 17, 1942, in Louisville, Kentucky. Descended from pre–Civil War American slaves, he grew up in a middle-class family. He had a younger brother, Rudy. His mother, Odessa, took her sons to church every Sunday. His father, Cassius Sr., was a hardworking sign painter. Like his son, he talked long and loud, telling stories, not all of them true.

Although slavery had been outlawed nearly one hundred years earlier, the Clays still faced racism. If Cassius Jr. went into a white neighborhood, people would call him names and tell him to leave. There were stores, restaurants, and hotels that black people could not use.

When Clay was 12, somebody stole his bike. He told a Louisville police officer he was going to "whup" the thief. The officer told him he should learn to fight first. Clay did, winning his first fight at 89 pounds a few weeks later. He eventually won six Kentucky Golden Gloves titles and two national Golden Gloves championships. He won more than 100 of his 108 amateur fights.

Clay loved to show off, but he did it in a way that made people laugh. At Louisville's Central High School during the late 1950s, he'd

After winning Olympic gold in Rome in 1960, Cassius returned to his Louisville high school to celebrate with friends.

walk the halls shadow boxing and saying he was getting ready to fight for the heavyweight championship.

Clay wasn't a good student. He graduated only because the high school principal liked him. Clay became a boxer because he thought it was the best and fastest way for a black person to become successful in America

During this time he became interested in a kind of religion different from that of his parents'. The Nation of Islam and its leader, Elijah Muhammad, talked about black pride, self-respect, and discipline. Muslims did not smoke, drink alcohol, or party. Elijah preached that blacks and whites should be separate. Other Nation ministers called white people "blue-eyed devils," which led some to think it was a religion of hate and violence. Another leader, Malcolm X, said that if white people hurt black people, then blacks should do the same to them.

Clay first heard about the Nation of Islam, also known as the Black Muslims, in 1959 while he was in Chicago for a Golden Gloves boxing tournament. Chicago was the headquarters for the Nation of Islam. An aunt came to Louisville with a record album of Elijah

Muhammad's sermons. Clay began reading the Nation's official newspaper, *Muhammad Speaks.*

Clay kept his interest to himself, although he did surprise his Central High School English teacher by saying he wanted to write his term paper on the Black Muslims. She would not allow it.

Meanwhile, his boxing was his number one interest. He did well enough to make the U.S. Olympic team. At age 18, Clay headed to the Summer Olympics in Rome, Italy. He was so afraid of flying, he took a parachute with him on the plane.

He loved walking around the Olympic Village and meeting athletes from all over the world. He quickly became so popular that people called him the Mayor of the Olympic Village.

Clay dominated the light heavyweight division. He easily won his first three fights. Then he beat Poland's Zbigniew Pietrzykowski to win the gold medal by unanimous decision. He strutted around the Olympic Village with his gold medal, never taking it off, even to sleep.

Still, he never forgot religion. After the 1960 Olympics, he attended Nation meetings. He kept his interest quiet because he thought if boxing people found out, they would not give him a shot at the heavyweight title.

His silence didn't last long.

Cassius won one of the United States' three boxing gold medals during the Rome Olympics. He won the light heavyweight division. The other U.S. boxing winners were Wilbert McClure and Eddie Crook.

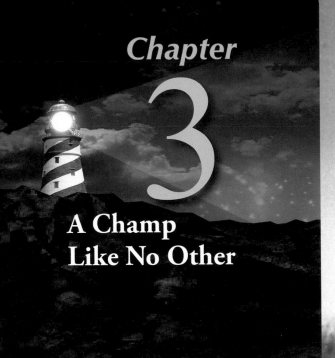

Chapter

3

A Champ Like No Other

It took just over three years before Clay got his championship shot after turning pro in 1960. He started predicting fights in April of 1961 while preparing to fight Lamar Clark, who had knocked out 45 straight opponents. Clay predicted he'd knock out Clark in two rounds, and he did just that.

Clay's talking earned him nicknames that included the Louisville Lip, Gaseous Cassius, Mighty Mouth, Cash the Brash, and more.

Clay turned his predictions into poems. Before fighting Archie Moore in November 1962, Clay said, "When you come to the fight, don't block the aisle and don't block the door. You will all go home after Round Four."

Clay could have knocked him out in three rounds, but he dragged it out to end the fight in four, just as he'd predicted.

Before beating Liston for the championship in 1964, the newly named Ali wrote a poem that included these lines: "The crowd did not dream when they laid down their money / that they would see a total eclipse of the Sonny."

Ali kept on winning easily before facing Ernie Terrell, who hadn't lost in five years. Terrell kept calling Ali "Clay," which angered the

newly converted Muslim. During the fight Ali would hit him and shout, "What's my name?"

Meanwhile, Ali had been drafted into the U.S. Army at the height of the Vietnam War. He refused to go because of religious reasons, saying, "War is against the teachings of the Holy Qur'an. I'm not trying to dodge the draft." The government responded by stripping him of his title and his ability to fight. He was sentenced to five years in prison and fined $10,000 for draft evasion. He appealed. Although the court dropped the prison sentence, it upheld the ban on boxing. For more than three years, Ali could not fight. He spent that time speaking out against the Vietnam war.

Finally, when he was 29, he was allowed to fight again. He won two fights to set up a battle with undefeated heavyweight champ Joe Frazier. Ali was also undefeated. Their March 8, 1971, battle at New York City's Madison Square Garden was called the Fight of the Century. Frazier won a unanimous decision.

Ali was down, but far from finished.

Muhammad knew how to win a crowd and he showed it in Zaire, Africa, before his heavyweight title fight there against George Foreman in 1974.

Ali had no chance. That's what everyone was saying in 1974. It was the year George Foreman loomed as boxing's Goliath. He was a huge man with punching power never seen before. He was 40–0 with 37 knockouts, and he had never been knocked down or hurt. He had 24 straight knockouts, and his last eight fights had lasted two rounds or less. Two of those were against Frazier. One was against top challenger Ken Norton, who had earlier beaten Ali after breaking his jaw.

Now it was Ali's turn. His fight doctor, Ferdie Pacheco, was so concerned about Ali getting hurt that he had a jet plane ready to take the fighter to a hospital specializing in brain injuries.

They called the fight the Rumble in the Jungle. It was staged in the African country of Zaire (now called the Democratic Republic of the Congo), with each fighter set to get a record $5 million.

Ali had waited three years for this fight. He had beaten Norton and Frazier to get this title shot, and he wasn't about to blow it.

Experts made Foreman a big favorite, just as they'd done with Sonny Liston eleven years earlier. Ali was older, bigger (as much as 236 pounds), and had lost the speed and fitness to dance for an entire fight.

But he had watched enough film of Foreman to believe he could tire him out—if he could take Foreman's power punching.

Foreman's plan was simple. "I was trying to destroy him," he said in a *USA Today* story.

Ali came to Zaire and quickly charmed the people. By the hot, humid night of the fight, October 30, 1974, Ali owned the crowd.

The ropes around the ring were loose, which allowed Ali to sag into them and help keep him away from the full power of Foreman's punches. He leaned into the ropes and let Foreman punch away, the blows and heat sapping Foreman's strength.

Ali called the strategy Rope a Dope, and round after round he let Foreman hit him, protecting his ribs and head with his arms and gloves. Ali's corner yelled at him to get off the ropes, but Ali knew what he was doing. Occasionally he would sting Foreman with a jab. As the rounds moved on, the jabs came faster, harder, and more often.

George Foreman was known for his power punching, but it was Muhammad who delivered a stunning knockout to regain the heavyweight championship.

Foreman had never been knocked down, let alone knocked out, as a professional. Muhammad did both thanks to his "rope a dope" strategy.

Finally, in the eighth round, Ali connected with a head shot and Foreman wobbled. Ali hit him again and again. The champ fell to the canvas, as much from fatigue and heat as from the power of Ali's punches. Ali had done the unthinkable: He won by a knockout.

After the fight, Foreman was bothered more by not knocking out Ali rather than losing. He couldn't believe anyone could take those punches.

Foreman and Ali became friends. Foreman tried to get Ali to retire before he got hurt, but Ali wouldn't do it. The pull of glory and limelight was too strong.

And, as it turned out, he had one great fight left.

Muhammad, former champ Joe Frazier and fight promoter Don King got together for one of the greatest fights in history. Frazier never forgave Muhammad for insulting him.

Manila Thrilla

Joe Frazier was washed up, done, a boxer past his prime. That's what Ali thought in 1975 as he prepared to face his rival for the third and last time. They would meet in the city of Manila in the Philippines. Like the first fight, this was for the heavyweight championship.

It was also personal.

Ali always insulted his opponents before fights, and he did not back off even though Frazier had beaten him once. He called Frazier "gorilla," "ugly," and "ignorant." Frazier was a proud man and the insults hurt. He vowed to make Ali pay.

More than 28,000 people packed into the Philippine Coliseum on a hot October night. Ali had gotten older and bigger, and his dancing had given way to flat-footed punching. Frazier fought as he always had, bobbing and weaving forward, always looking to throw the brutal left hook that had crumpled Ali in their first fight.

Ali looked unbeatable in the first three rounds, and Frazier's face swelled from all the punches. But in the fourth round he began getting to Ali, hitting him with shots he later told *Sports Illustrated* "would have knocked down a wall." In the sixth round, Frazier rocked Ali with two vicious left hooks that would have knocked out a lesser fighter.

Frazier had one style, attack at all times, which meant getting in harm's way of Muhammad's punches.

To start the seventh round, Ali said, according to *Sports Illustrated,* "Old Joe Frazier, I thought you was washed up." Frazier replied, "Somebody told you wrong, pretty boy."

After ten rounds, the fight was even. Frazier battered Ali in the 11th round. Ali returned the favor in the 12th, and by the 13th Frazier's mouth was bleeding. His punches lost their power. His eyes were swollen nearly shut, and he could no longer protect himself. Ali hit him with nine straight rights.

After the round, Frazier's manager, Eddie Futch, told him he was going to stop the fight. Frazier begged him not to do it, but Futch saw what Frazier could not.

The fight was over.

Many said Ali should have retired, but he fought 10 more times. He lost his title to Leon Spinks, then regained it from Spinks. He retired, then came back to fight two more times despite pleas from his team doctor to stop. After getting knocked out in both of those fights, he retired for good in 1981. His record was 56–5. He was the first man to hold the heavyweight title three different times.

Yet, he still had to face his toughest opponent of all.

Muhammad met many famous people in his career. Top left: He jokes around with the Beatles. Top right: Muhammad with singer Bob Dylan. Bottom left: He has fun with pop band the Jackson Five. Bottom right: Muhammad with civil rights leader Malcolm X and Malcolm's daughters.

One of the most dramatic moments of the 1996 Olympic Games in Atlanta came when Muhammad surprised everyone by appearing to light the Olympic flame to start the games.

Glory Beyond
the Ring

Ali stood in the shadows, the song "Sweet Georgia Brown" playing in the background, as excited as he'd ever been for a championship fight. It was July 19, 1996, and he was in Atlanta to light the torch to start the Summer Olympic Games. His hands shook noticeably, partly from nerves, mostly from Parkinson's disease, but he didn't care.

Olympic officials had kept his appearance a secret. When he appeared, dressed in white, the roar from the Olympic Stadium was deafening. He raised the torch in his right hand and the crowd roared louder. For a moment, he was king of the world again. According to a *New Yorker* story, afterward he sat for hours in his hotel room holding the torch. He looked as if he had won the heavyweight title for a fourth time.

He had learned to live with Parkinson's disease, which affects people no matter how famous or rich they are. It attacks the nervous system and stiffens the muscles. It causes the hands to shake and takes away a person's ability to speak.

Ali began showing symptoms shortly before he retired. In 1984, he was officially diagnosed with Parkinson's. All the blows to the head over the years likely caused the disease. His ability to take a punch, so valuable in the ring, had left permanent brain damage.

Despite his illness, Ali stayed busy. He went on goodwill missions to North Korea and Afghanistan, and he helped deliver medical supplies to Cuba. He went to South Africa to meet Nelson Mandela after the great civil rights leader was released from prison. He also took part in the opening ceremonies of the 2012 Summer Olympics in London.

Muhammad was inspired by South Africa civil rights leader Nelson Mandela, who had been unjustly imprisoned for nearly 30 years, and flew to South Africa to meet him after Mandela's release.

Ali has helped such organizations as the Special Olympics and the Make-A-Wish Foundation. Louisville's Muhammad Ali Center gives out annual humanitarian awards. Ali tried to help President Barrack Obama become more popular by having his picture taken with him. While many celebrities avoid fans, he would go to restaurants to sign autographs or talk. He would visit nursing homes to help make residents smile or laugh. He would go to hospitals and soup kitchens. He loved it when he was recognized.

Muhammad always enjoys meeting people. Here he has fun while visiting the Special Olympics.

Ali is one of the most honored athletes in history. *Sports Illustrated* named him its Sportsman of the Century. So did *GQ* magazine and the British Broadcast Company. Ali has made the cover of *Sports Illustrated* 37 times, second only to Michael Jordan (50 covers).

Ali has been married four times. He has been married to his fourth wife, Yolanda "Lonnie" Williams, since 1986. They had been friends since the 1960s. He has seven daughters (Maryum, Jamillah, Rasheda, Hana, Laila, Miya, and Khaliah) and two sons (Muhammad Jr. and Asaad Amin).

Laila also became a professional boxer, although Ali didn't like it (even though she was 24–0 through 2014) because he didn't think women should fight. Maryum has been a rapper and an author.

Ali has homes in Michigan; Louisville, Kentucky; and Scottsdale, Arizona.

Ali made an album of spoken words in 1963 called *I Am the Greatest.* He first appeared in a movie in 1962, in which he had a small role, playing himself in *Requiem for a Heavyweight.* He appeared in a documentary film called *Black Rodeo,* in which he rode a horse and a bull. In 1978, he starred in the TV movie *Freedom Road,* playing an ex-slave who was elected to the U.S. Senate in the 1870s. He also starred in a 1969 Broadway musical called *Buck White.*

Twice in 2014, family members said Ali was in bad health and might not make it. But three of his daughters said that while their then 72-year-old father struggled to walk and talk, he wasn't dying. He joked that he was going to win back the title for the fourth time. He was at peace and not in pain, a legend as much for his role in civil rights and the 1960s' anti-war movement as for his boxing.

Through it all Ali continued to watch his old fight films when he was young and strong and invincible, when he was the king of the world.

- United Nations Messenger of Peace, 1998–2008, for his work with developing nations
- Presidential Medal of Freedom in 2005, the United States of America's highest civil award
- Amnesty International's Lifetime Achievement Award
- Germany's 2005 Otto Hahn Peace Medal, for his involvement in the U.S. civil rights movement and the United Nations
- International Ambassador of Jubilee 2000, a global organization dedicated to relieving debt in developing nations
- State of Kentucky's "Kentuckian of the Century"
- The Advertising Club of Louisville's Louisvillian of the Century

Other honors include an Essence Award, an XNBA Human Spirit Award, and recognition from the National Urban League; 100 Black Men; Givat Haviva; the Oleander Foundation; The National Conference of Christians and Jews; and *TIME* magazine.

	Opponent	Outcome	Length	Date
Win	Tunney Hunsaker	Decision (unanimous)	6 (6)	10/29/1960
Win	Herb Siler	KO	4 (8)	12/27/1960
Win	Tony Esperti	TKO	3 (8), 1:30	01/17/1961
Win	Jimmy Robinson	KO	1 (8), 1:34	02/07/1961
Win	Donnie Fleeman	TKO	7 (8)	02/21/1961
Win	LaMar Clark	KO	2 (10), 1:27	04/19/1961
Win	Duke Sabedong	Decision (unanimous)	10 (10)	06/26/1961
Win	Alonzo Johnson	Decision (unanimous)	10 (10)	07/22/1961
Win	Alex Miteff	TKO	6 (10), 1:45	10/07/1961
Win	Willi Besmanoff	TKO	7 (10), 1:55	11/29/1961
Win	Sonny Banks	TKO	4 (10), 0:26	02/10/1962
Win	Don Warner	TKO	4, 0:34	02/28/1962
Win	George Logan	TKO	4 (10), 1:34	04/23/1962
Win	Billy Daniels	TKO	7 (10), 2:21	05/19/1962
Win	Alejandro Lavorante	KO	5 (10), 1:48	07/20/1962
Win	Archie Moore	TKO	4 (10), 1:35	11/15/1962
Win	Charlie Powell	KO	3, 2:04	01/24/1963
Win	Doug Jones	Decision (unanimous)	10 (10)	03/13/1963
Win	Henry Cooper	TKO	5 (10), 2:15	06/18/1963
Win	Sonny Liston	TKO	7 (15)	02/25/1964
Win	Sonny Liston	KO	1 (15), 2:12	05/25/1965

Win	Floyd Patterson	TKO	12 (15), 2:18	11/22/1965
Win	George Chuvalo	Decision (unanimous)	15 (15)	03/29/1966
Win	Henry Cooper	TKO	6 (15), 1:38	05/21/1966
Win	Brian London	KO	3 (15)	08/06/1966
Win	Karl Mildenberger	TKO	12 (15)	09/10/1966
Win	Cleveland Williams	TKO	3 (15)	11/14/1966
Win	Ernie Terrell	Decision (unanimous)	15 (15)	02/06/1967
Win	Zora Folley	KO	7 (15), 1:48	03/22/1967
Win	Jerry Quarry	TKO	3 (15)	10/26/1970
Win	Oscar Bonavena	TKO	15 (15), 2:03	12/07/1970
Loss	Joe Frazier	Decision (unanimous)	15 (15)	03/08/1971
Win	Jimmy Ellis	TKO	12 (12), 2:10	07/26/1971
Win	Buster Mathis	Decision (unanimous)	12 (12)	11/17/1971
Win	Jürgen Blin	KO	7 (12), 2:12	12/26/1971
Win	Mac Foster	Decision (unanimous)	15 (15)	04/01/1972
Win	George Chuvalo	Decision (unanimous)	12 (12)	05/01/1972
Win	Jerry Quarry	TKO	7 (12), 0:19	06/27/1972
Win	Alvin Lewis	TKO	11 (12), 1:15	07/19/1972
Win	Floyd Patterson	TKO	7 (12)	09/20/1972
Win	Bob Foster	KO	7 (12)	11/21/1972
Win	Joe Bugner	Decision (unanimous)	12 (12)	02/14/1973
Loss	Ken Norton	Decision (split)	12 (12)	03/31/1973
Win	Ken Norton	Decision (split)	12 (12)	09/10/1973
Win	Rudi Lubbers	Decision (unanimous)	12 (12)	10/20/1973
Win	Joe Frazier	Decision (unanimous)	12 (12)	01/28/1974
Win	George Foreman	KO	8 (15), 2:58	10/30/1974
Win	Chuck Wepner	TKO	15 (15), 2:41	03/24/1975
Win	Ron Lyle	TKO	11 (15)	05/16/1975
Win	Joe Bugner	Decision (unanimous)	15 (15)	06/30/1975
Win	Joe Frazier	TKO	14 (15), 0:59	10/01/1975
Win	Jean-Pierre Coopman	KO	5 (15)	02/20/1976
Win	Jimmy Young	Decision (unanimous)	15 (15)	04/30/1976
Win	Richard Dunn	TKO	5 (15)	05/24/1976
Win	Ken Norton	Decision (unanimous)	15 (15)	09/28/1976
Win	Alfredo Evangelista	Decision (unanimous)	15 (15)	05/16/1977
Win	Earnie Shavers	Decision (unanimous)	15 (15)	09/29/1977
Loss	Leon Spinks	Decision (split)	15 (15)	02/15/1978
Win	Leon Spinks	Decision (unanimous)	15 (15)	09/15/1978
Loss	Larry Holmes	TKO	10 (15)	10/02/1980
Loss	Trevor Berbick	Decision (unanimous)	10 (10)	12/11/1981

Books

Ali, Hana Yasmeen and Muhammad. *The Soul of a Butterfly: Reflections on Life's Journey.* New York: Simon & Schuster, 2013.

Arkush, Michael. *The Fight of the Century: Ali vs. Frazier, March 8, 1971.* New York: Wiley, 2007.

Hauser, Thomas. *Muhammad Ali: His Life and Times.* New York: Simon & Schuster, 1992.

Myers, Walter Dean. *The Greatest: Muhammad Ali.* New York: Scholastic Paperbacks, 2001.

Remnick, David. *King of the World: Muhammad Ali and the Rise of an American Hero.* New York: 1st Vintage Books, 1999.

Taschen. *Greatest of All Time: A Tribute to Muhammad Ali.* Cologne, Germany, 2010.

West, David. *The Mammoth Book of Muhammad Ali.* London: Robinson Publishing, 2012.

Works Consulted

Kram, Mark. "Lawdy, Lawdy, He's Great." *Sports Illustrated*, 1975.

Miller, David. "My Dinner with Ali." *Sport Magazine,* 1989

Muhammad Ali Lights Torch

http://sports.espn.go.com/espn/espn25/story?page=moments/8

Muhammad Ali quotes.

http://communitytable.com/264190/vianguyen/50th-anniversary-of-liston-clay-fi ght-15-ofmuhammad-alis-best-quotes/

Official Muhammad Ali web site.

http://www.ali.com/

Peter, Josh. "Muhammad Ali's condition not so dire, his daughters say." *USA Today,* October 30, 2014.

http://www.usatoday.com/story/sports/boxing/2014/10/29/muhammad-ali-parkinsons-diseaserumble-in-the-jungle/18146549/

Peter, Josh. "Revisiting 'The Rumble in the Jungle' 40 years later," *USA Today,* October 30, 2014.

http://www.usatoday.com/story/sports/boxing/2014/10/29/muhammad-ali-george-foremanrumble-in-the-jungle-40th-anniversary/18097587/

Remnick David. "American Hunger." *The New Yorker,* October 12, 1998.

http://www.newyorker.com/magazine/1998/10/12/american-hunger

Walden, Celia. "Don't pity our father Muhammad Ali. He's happy.' *The Telegraph,* December 15, 2014.

http://www.telegraph.co.uk/culture/fi lm/11290317/Dont-pity-our-father-Muhammed-Ali.-Heshappy.html

On the Internet

Muhammad Ali

http://www.ducksters.com/biography/athletes/muhammad_ali.php

Muhammad Ali

http://www.history.com/topics/black-history/muhammad-ali

Muhammad Ali Biography for Kids

http://mrnussbaum.com/athletes/muhammed_ali/

Muhammad Ali Facts

https://kidskonnect.com/people/muhammad-ali/

Muhammad Ali Mini Bio (Video)

https://www.youtube.com/watch?v=jIxbhA4su0g

GLOSSARY

amateur (AM-uh-chur)—Someone who does not make money from a sport, hobby, or other activity.

corner men—In boxing, the coaches or trainers who help a fighter during a fight. They might give water, treat cuts or bruises, and give advice and encouragement.

documentary (dah-kyoo-MEN-tuh-ree)—An educational film that tells true fact-filled stories.

drafted—Selected by the government to join the military.

draft evasion (ee-VAY-zhun)—Taking action, such as moving to another country, to avoid serving in the military.

Golden Gloves—An amateur boxing organization that holds local, state, and national tournaments.

Goliath (goh-LY-uth)—A very large person. In the Bible, Goliath was a giant warrior defeated by David.

heavyweight championship (HEH-vee-wayt CHAM-pyun-ship)—A fight to determine who is the best in the heaviest weight division.

humanitarian (hyoo-man-ih-TAYR-ee-un)—A person who is concerned about or helps other people.

jab—In boxing, a punch that strikes suddenly and sharply.

knockout (NOK-owt)—In boxing, hitting someone hard enough that they fall down and cannot get up before the count of 10.

mobster—A criminal who is part of an organized gang.

Olympics (oh-LIM-piks)—An international sporting event held every four years that brings together the world's athletes to determine who is the best in each particular sport.

Parkinson's disease (PAR-kin-sonz dih-ZEEZ)—An illness that produces tremors, muscle weakness, difficulty in walking, and a slowness in movement.

professional (proh-FEH-shuh-nul)—Someone who makes money from a sport or other activity.

promote (pruh-MOHT)—To create interest in a person or event.

racism (RAY-sih-zum)—The belief that a person or people from a particular race or group is not equal to another.

requiem (REH-kwee-um)—A religious song or service for the dead.

shadow box—To spar with an imaginary opponent as a form of training.

spar—To make the motions of boxing without landing heavy blows, as a form of training.

unanimous (yoo-NAN-uh-mus)—Agreed by an entire group.

Viet Cong (vee-et KONG)—A military group that fought the United States and the South Vietnamese during the Vietnam War.

Vietnam War (vee-et-NAHM)—The war that was fought in Southeast Asia from the 1960s into the 1970s. The United States fought with the Vietnamese people in the south against the Viet Cong in the north. Vietnam was finally divided into two separate countries.